GRADUATED REPERTOIRE FOR THE CLASSICAL GUITARIST

BOOK 2

COMPILED AND EDITED BY
JEFFREY MCFADDEN AND
ANDREW ZOHN

Production: Frank J. Hackinson
Editor, Production Coordinator: Philip Groeber
Cover Design: Adrianne Hirosky
Engraving: Tempo Music Press, Inc.
Printer: Tempo Music Press, Inc.

ISBN-13: 978-1-56939-657-5

ABOUT THE SERIES

Welcome to *Graduated Repertoire for the Classical Guitarist*. In these pages we have attempted to compile some of the most engaging and technically satisfying music for the developing guitarist and arrange it progressively, page by page. You will find some of the great, proven pieces from the standard didactic repertoire as well as a wealth of exciting new material arranged in a carefully graded format. This series blends Renaissance, Baroque, Classical, and Romantic styles, with a strong presence of Contemporary, World Music, and Folk music pieces.

In the early volumes especially, emphasis has been placed both on musical quality and playability. As teachers are aware, students (and even professionals) respond to repertoire both in an aural and a tactile way. A piece that is not only musically enticing, but also fun to play, is more likely to be practiced thoroughly.
Our hope is that through the page-by-page study of the early volumes particularly, the student will develop first and foremost a secure and stable right-hand technique. Many of the first pieces can be performed with totally stable finger-string associations. Alternation and string crossing techniques are introduced progressively. Similarly, left-hand challenges are introduced progressively; there are very few position shifts, slurs, or barres required in the early volumes and each of these techniques is addressed gradually, once left-hand stability has been established.

While there is an underlying pedagogical philosophy in the selection and ordering of the repertoire in these volumes, the series is not intended as a method. We recommend that the students be guided through a beginner's method to develop the rudiments of musical literacy and technical know-how prior to embarking on the repertoire contained in these volumes. After an initial phase of establishing these basics, *Graduated Repertoire for the Classical Guitarist* may be used as a source of repertoire to reinforce ideas and techniques introduced in an ongoing and multi-faceted process of study.

An important feature of *Graduated Repertoire for the Classical Guitarist* is the inclusion of written directions for each piece. These short statements describe the character or historical context of the piece and help in pinpointing special technical issues and challenges. They are intended as a friendly voice to help guide the student.

We have worked to present an ordered and very carefully fingered selection of repertoire for the developing guitarist, but we acknowledge that there are "many ways to skin a cat"— many valid ways to approach the study of the guitar. The experienced teacher is therefore encouraged to reorder the pieces and change fingerings as they see fit.

We truly hope that these volumes can provide a framework for organized, productive study, help the developing guitarist become familiar with the panorama of guitar repertoire, and provide the opportunity for fun in learning. At the end, we hope that users of *Graduated Repertoire for the Classical Guitarist* will have been helped along the path to the great joy of playing the guitar and playing it well!

Jeffrey McFadden
Andrew Zohn

TABLE OF CONTENTS

G1039

G1039

Estudio

Andrew Zohn
(b. 1970)

In this etude, all of the fingers alternate singularly against *p*.
Be sure to hold down pivot fingers in the left hand where the
same note is needed in different harmonies, such as the A on
the third string in measures 1-3.

Ode to Joy

This is an arrangement of what is perhaps Beethoven's best-loved melody. This piece requires free alternation of *i* and *m*, as introduced in Book 1. Make sure that one finger extends outward in preparation as the other finger strikes. To avoid tension in the right hand, be careful to have *a* and *c* (the little finger) move along side of *m* while alternating.

Ludwig van Beethoven
(1770–1827)
arr. Andrew Zohn
(b. 1970)

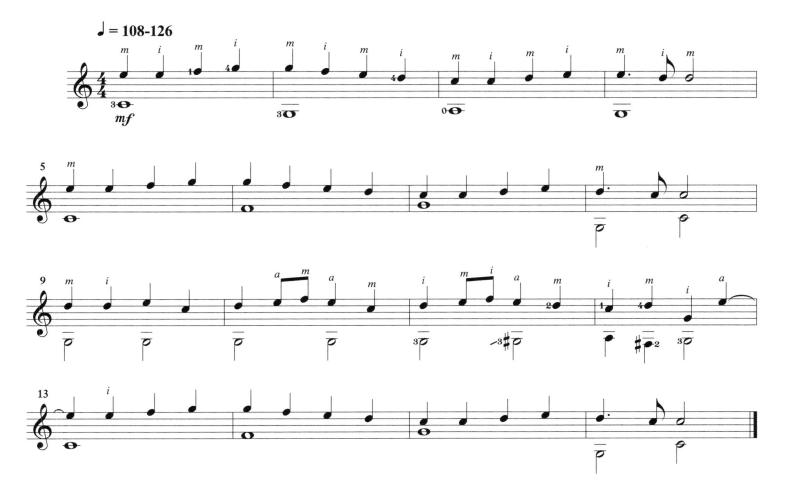

Moderato

This is a simple selection from the great Romantic era composer, J.K. Mertz. It is technically very accessible but presents a rhythmic challenge. Aim to switch comfortably from triplets to duplets and back again while maintaining a steady tempo. Some practice with the metronome will be very useful here!

Johan Kaspar Mertz
(1806–1856)

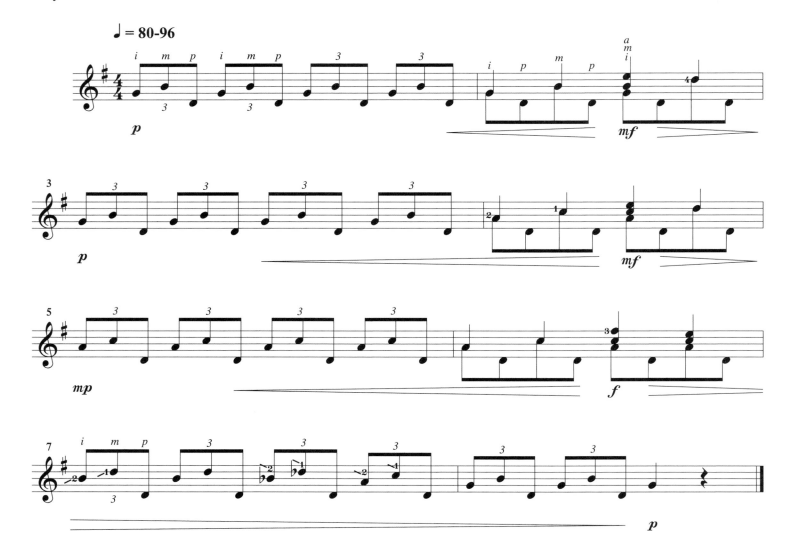

Rush Hour in Huronia

(Huron Carol)

This composition features three reiterations of the melody of the *Huron Carol*, the first in the key of a minor and the second and third (starting in measure 17) in the contrasting key of e minor. The right hand is required to alternate between *p* and *m*, and also between *i* and *m*.

Traditional Folk Song
arr. Jeffrey McFadden
(b. 1963)

Tribute

Jeffrey McFadden
(b. 1963)

This piece features motivic characteristics of the music of
the great Cuban composer Leo Brouwer. Measures 19-21 are
a favorite Bulgarian tune of Brouwer's. Be sure to follow
sound principles of right-hand alternation.

Waltz No. 1
(from *Op. 59*)

Matteo Carcassi
(1792–1853)

This fun waltz integrates several techniques learned in earlier parts of this series. As always, follow the given dynamic indications and work to create an interesting interpretation. Note especially that the first section should be executed with strong and clearly defined dynamic contrast between opposing phrases.

Folías

Traditional
arr. Jeffrey McFadden
(b. 1963)

This is a very well-known and much-loved harmonic pattern from ancient Western musical tradition. It has served as the theme for very many sets of variations. In guitar literature, the variations of Giuliani, Sor, and Ponce are excellent examples. Be sure to observe the rests in the bass.

Tremolino Etude

This composition is centered around the right-hand finger patterns *p-a-m* and *p-a-m-i*; the latter of which is the pattern commonly employed in famous works by such noted composers as Tárrega, Barrios, and Rodrigo to name a few. In order to execute this pattern effectively, *i, m,* and *a* should move out beyond the given string together (with *i* extended the furthest) at the instant that *p* sounds its note. Then one after another, each finger should engage and follow through the string.

Andrew Zohn
(b. 1970)

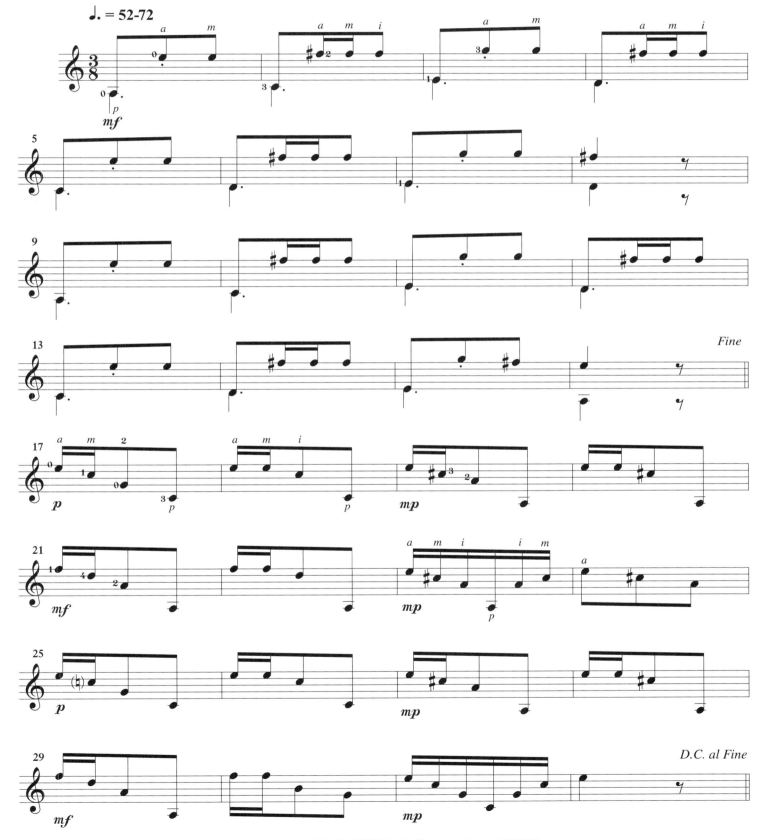

G1039

Andante No. 1

This piece features an arpeggio pattern in the second section, which requires *p* to strike multiple strings. In measure 19, the *i* finger should stay in the vicinity of the third string, and *p* should extend and contract to strike the assigned notes. Be sure not to move the entire arm and hand upward to place *p* but rather, move *p* independently.

Ferdinando Carulli
(1770–1841)

Sur le pont d'Avignon

(On the Bridge at Avignon)

Traditional
arr. Jeffrey McFadden
(b. 1963)

This setting of an ancient French folk tune features the migration of the melody to the bass voice in measure 17. Pay special attention to the dotted rhythms and work towards perfect fluency in the challenging measures 14-15.

G1039

Homesick
(Un Canadien errant)

This is an arrangement of a well-loved Canadian folk song about longing for one's homeland while living in exile. Take note of the left-hand fingering in measure 21 and of the rhythm at the end of the piece.

Traditional Canadian Folk Song
arr. Jeffrey McFadden
(b. 1963)

Las palmas

Jeffrey McFadden
(b. 1963)

This piece is in the style of South American works which are an integral part of the concert guitar repertoire. Note that the rests must be observed literally for stylistic reasons, and most especially when there are rests in both voices (for example, on the third quarter-note beat of measures 1, 5, 9, etc.). The tempo marking is given here in half-notes and the piece should ultimately be performed with these longer pulses, but it is advisable to play in slower, quarter-note beats as you are learning the piece.

Allegretto

This classic piece is a good preliminary exercise in the execution of implied counterpoint, a term which describes the illusion of more than one voice being present in a single-lined melody. In this piece, notes with upward stems should be treated as a separate melody from those that are down-stemmed only. This can be easily accomplished by playing the upward stemmed notes slightly louder than the others, and as *legato* as possible.

Ferdinando Carulli
(1770–1841)

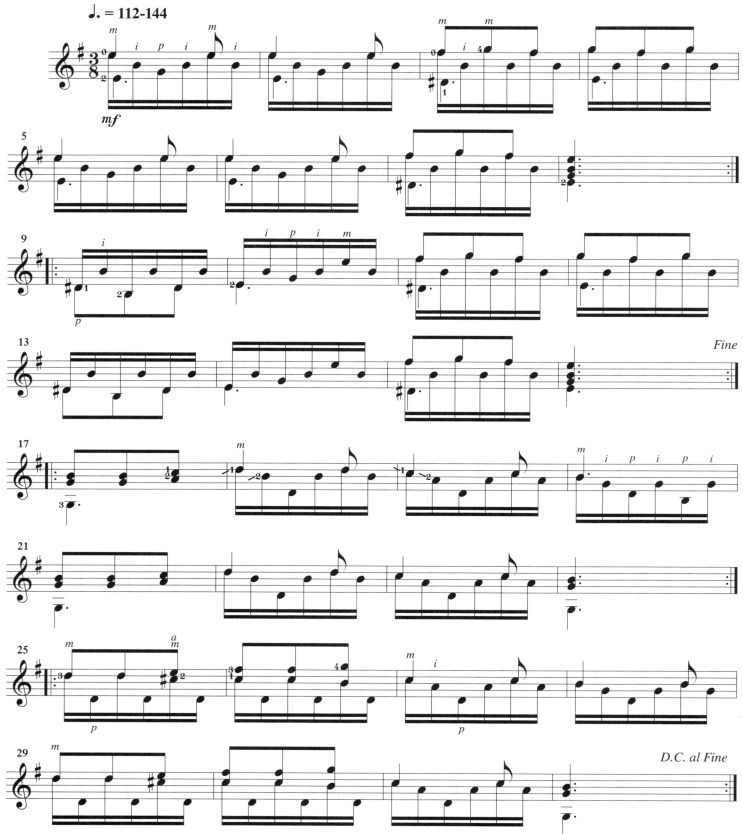

Sun Dance

from *Elementary Studies for Guitar, Book 2*

Shawn Bell
(b. 1958)

This character piece by the Canadian composer Shawn Bell features a continuously syncopated rhythm in which some of the strongest beats of the bar have no articulated notes. The right hand features alternation across adjacent strings (similar to the Carcassi *Andantino* in Book 1) and the left hand is best played with "fixed" fingers in some places (in measure 9 and the following several bars, the second and third fingers should stay on their notes). Also, take note of the change in arpeggio pattern in measure 17.

Tempura

Jeffrey McFadden
(b. 1963)

This piece uses a similar *arpeggio* pattern to the *Prelude* by Carcassi in Book 1. It serves as a wonderful example of how harmony can be created by moving a left-hand chord form around the fretboard of the guitar, a technique explored most famously by Heitor Villa-Lobos. Note that in measures 9, 11, and 14, some of the B notes are played open on the second string while others are played on the third.

Waltz No. 3

(from *Op. 59*)

Matteo Carcassi
(1792–1853)

This piece features some contrary motion at the beginning of the second section (measures 11-13). Contrary motion describes the occurrence of two voices simultaneously moving in opposite directions. To define the integrity of both lines, first play each voice separately and then play them together.

Sciapodus

Count carefully as you learn this piece to memorize the rhythmic flow or "groove." The texture involves simple alternation in the upper voice and an ostinato in the bass. The title, *Sciapodus*, (Sci-a-PO-dus) refers to a creature or being with huge feet!

Shawn Bell
(b. 1958)

Nativity

(Il est né le divin enfant)

Traditional
arr. Jeffrey McFadden
(b. 1963)

This simple and beautiful French carol is set here with a reprise in natural harmonics (measures 19-20 and 23-24). Follow the suggested right-hand fingering carefully, and be sure to give bass notes their full duration to create the desired texture in the music.

Romantic Waltz

Andrew Zohn
(b. 1970)

Make sure to bring out the melody in this piece by playing the upward-stemmed notes clearly and with a *legato* articulation. The complicated left-hand changes in measures 22-25 can be made easier by holding the fourth finger on the high G, using it as a pivot finger.

Bonnie Jean's Song

This piece features lush, jazz-like harmonies set upon a simple *arpeggio* pattern. The term *sostenuto* at the beginning of the piece suggests that notes should be allowed to ring as long as possible. To enhance the harmonic color of each measure, be sure to not only hold notes in the bass for their full value, but also let any other note ring for as long as it is practical to do so.

Andrew Zohn
(b. 1970)

The Messenger's Pavan

(D'où viens-tu bergère?)
(Where Have You Come From, Shepherd Girl?)

This is an arrangement of a beautiful French Canadian Christmas carol. Note the important *meno mosso* in measure 17 and take special care to follow the suggested left-hand fingering from this measure until the end.

Traditional
arr. Jeffrey McFadden
(b. 1963)

Theme from The William Tell Overture

This is a simple arrangement of the famous overture from Rossini's opera. Note that the piece is set here in *alla breve* time (**2/2**) and should be played at a fast tempo. Follow the fingering suggestions carefully as it will be especially important here to have an organized right-hand approach.

Gioacchino Rossini
(1792–1868)
arr. Jeffrey McFadden
(b. 1963)

Maracatu

Andrew Zohn
(b. 1970)

This stylized Latin dance continues the right-hand technical challenge of alternation with *i* and *m*. Be careful to bring out the inherent syncopation of the second section by giving all notes in the treble and bass their full values.

Allegro

Carl Blum
(1786–1844)

This piece is from a collection of studies by the German singer, composer, and guitarist, Carl Blum, and is designed to highlight left-hand techniques. Be sure to maintain the third finger on low G from measures 4-6 and note the shift in positions in measures 9-10 and measures 14-15. Advanced players can try a two-string barre and subsequent pivot in these measures to avoid jumping finger 1 from the first to the second string.

Andante

This charming miniature introduces the concept of *scordatura* to this series. In order to sound the low pedal point D in the bass, one must tune the sixth string down by one whole step. This is most commonly achieved by matching the lowered string to the open fourth string, which will then be one octave apart.

Anton Diabelli
(1781–1858)

Angels We Have Heard on High

Be sure to pay specific attention to the right-hand fingerings in the eighth-note descending scale passages. There are other workable fingering combinations for these passages, but the strict alternation of the fingers is a must.

Traditional French Carol
arr. Andrew Zohn
(b. 1970)

G1039

Etude

This etude is an excellent introduction to reading in the second position. Be sure to follow the left-hand fingerings, as they were derived to accommodate the right-hand alternation of *i* and *m* wherever possible.

Francisco Tárrega
(1852–1909)

Andante No. 2

(Opus 241, No. 5)

Ferdinando Carulli
(1770–1841)

This charming piece provides an excellent example of parallel motion against a pedal point (the G in measures 1-4), a common texture in classical-period music. Be sure to emphasize the overlapping voices in measures 7 and 10 by holding every note for its full duration.

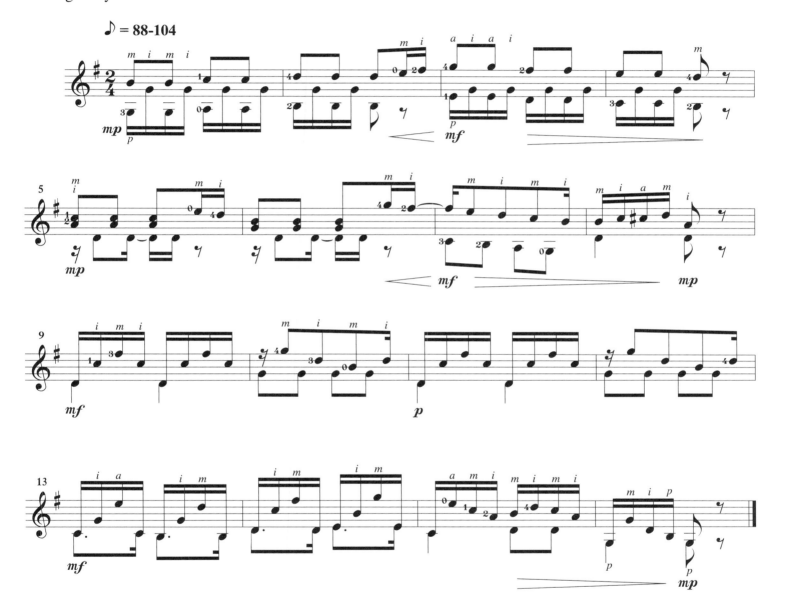

GLOSSARY

ad lib

An abbreviation for *ad libitum*, allowing the performer to vary the tempo or improvise.

alla breve

A term describing the 2/2 time signature. It suggests that the music should be performed and perceived as the half note receiving one beat as opposed to the quarter note. The term has its origin in early music notation systems.

a niente

A *diminuendo* that fades until nothing is heard.

Allegro non troppo

Fast, not too much.

Andantino

A little faster than *andante*.

a tempo

Return to the original tempo, especially after a *rit*.

barre

The use of one of the left-hand fingers (almost always the first finger) in a flattened or straight position to cover more than one string at a time.

bransle

A dance of the Renaissance. It appears in a variety of forms, some in two beat patterns, others in patterns of three beats. The example in this volume is taken from one of the earliest guitar tablature books printed in 16th century France.

contrary motion

This occurs when two voice parts move simultaneously in different directions.

counterpoint

Music in which two or more independent lines sound simultaneously.

e

The Italian word for "and".

Etude/Estudio

The French and Spanish terms for "study," a short piece written for didactic or teaching purposes.

glissando

The process of sliding a finger or fingers up or down a string of the instrument. On the guitar, the technique involves shifting the left hand without releasing the pressure of the fingers on the fingerboard. The musical result is a sliding, continuous change of pitch, often called a *portamento* or "carrying" of the pitch. The effect is used frequently in later 19th century guitar repertoire as well as in contemporary and folk music.

grace note

A small ornamental note placed before a principal note. Play the grace note quickly before the main note.

grazioso

Grace, gracefully.

harmonics

A technique where a string is lightly touched at a certain fret (node), producing a higher bell-like tone, or harmonic.

Huronia

The ancestral lands of the Hurons, an aboriginal tribe of central North America.

Key of a minor

The tonal center of the piece is A. The key signature is the same as the Relative Major Key of C, with no sharps or flats in the key signature.

l.v.

(laissez vibrer) Let vibrate.

marcato il basso

Mark or stress the bass notes.

maracatu	A stylized Latin dance originating in the Pernambuco state of northeastern Brazil.
meno mosso	Less motion or less quickly.
meter	A regular pattern of beats which comprise measures.
metronome	A device which sounds regular beats indicating the tempo or speed of the piece. For example: ♩ = 120 means that the tempo is 120 quarter notes per minute 𝅗𝅥 = 120 indicates *alla breve* time where a half note receives one beat, or 120 half notes per minute. ♪ =120 means that the tempo is 120 eighth notes per minute
milonga	A popular dance from the late 19th century in South America.
minimalist texture	Minimalism is a movement in music with origins in the mid-20th century where very sparing musical motives were repeated with small elements of variety gradually added to develop the musical materials and create form. The effect of minimalist music is often experienced as "hypnotic." Minimalist textures can be found in the guitar music of Leo Brouwer.
molto	An Italian term for much, or very. *Rit. molto* means a large or exaggerated *ritard*.
morendo	Fading away. Literally, dying.
ostinato	A recognizable pattern that is continuously repeated.
parallel motion	Occurs when two voice parts move in the same direction.
pedal point	A bass note which is played or sustained while the harmonies change in the upper parts.
pivot finger	Keeping a left-hand finger in place as other left-hand fingers are moving.
poco	A little. *Poco rit.* means a little *ritard*.
rall.	An abbreviation for *rallentando* which means the same as *rit.*, a gradual slowing down of the tempo.
scordatura	The non-standard tuning of a stringed instrument.
simile	Continue in the same way.
slur	A curved line connecting two or more notes indicating a hammer-on (ascending notes) or pull-off (descending notes).
sostenuto	Sustaining the tone.
syncopation	An accent on a weak beat or between beats.
terms of form	*D.C. al Coda* = return to the beginning of the piece and then proceed to the *Coda* (⊕) *D.S. al Coda* = return to the *Segno* (sign) 𝄋 and then proceed to the *Coda* (⊕) *D.S. al Fine* = return to the *Segno* (sign) 𝄋 and then end at the word *Fine* *To Coda* (⊕) = a direction in the music indicating to proceed to the *Coda* (⊕) *Coda* (⊕) = the ending section of a piece *Fine* (FEE-nay)= the final end of the piece
waltz	A dance in a moderate triple meter.

ABOUT THE COMPOSERS

Ludwig van Beethoven (1770–1827) was one of the most influential composers of all time. Beethoven was born into a musical family in Bonn, Germany. As a young man he studied piano with Joseph Haydn and ultimately became a virtuoso pianist. During his lifetime he composed nine symphonies and several concerti along with many important chamber works and sonatas for solo piano. He continued to compose and conduct in spite of progressive hearing loss.

Shawn Bell (b. 1958) is a Canadian composer, an educator, and new media professional. Dedicated to creativity, he has taught creative arts for ages ranging from kindergarten to college students. Bell has performed as a solo guitarist, in small ensembles, and in collaboration with dancers and theatre troupes. As a guitar teacher, he began composing pieces specifically for the technical and musical needs of his students. Many of his compositions have been used in film and television.

Carl Blum (1786–1844) was a student of Antonio Salieri. Blum wrote an extensive body of solo guitar music and chamber music with guitar. His music possesses a dramatic, bright and lively quality, a reflection of his extensive studies and work in theater and opera. He served as Royal Composer of the Royal Opera in Berlin and in other important positions during his extensive and varied career.

Matteo Carcassi (1792–1853) was born in Italy. Carcassi moved to Germany in 1810, gaining almost immediate success. From 1820 on, he spent the majority of his time in Paris, but traveled to London where he gained a reputation as both a teacher and concert artist. Carcassi wrote an instructional method for guitar (Op. 59) that remains valuable, relevant and interesting.

Ferdinando Carulli (1770–1841) was a gifted performer. Carulli was born in Naples, Italy and devoted his life to the study and advancement of the guitar. As there were no professional guitar teachers in Naples at the time, Carulli developed his own style of playing and wrote a classical guitar method that is still used today.

Anton Diabelli (1781–1858) was an Austrian music publisher, editor, and composer who studied music before entering Raitenhaslach Abbey in 1800. After the disbanding of the Bavarian monasteries in 1803 he went to Vienna, where he taught the piano and guitar.

Johann Kaspar Mertz (1806–1856) was a Hungarian virtuoso guitarist and composer. His guitar music was unique, following pianistic models of the time rather than the classical or bel canto styles favored by other guitar composers. The *Bardenklänge* (1847) are probably Mertz's most important contribution to the guitar repertoire— a series of deceptively easy character pieces written in the style of Schumann.

Gioacchino Rossini (1792–1868) was born in Italy. Rossini composed 39 operas, as well as sacred music and chamber music. The overture to his opera *William Tell* is one of the most famous and frequently recorded works in the classical repertoire. His tendency to use song-like melodies earned him the nickname "The Italian Mozart."

Francisco Tárrega (1852–1909) was an influential Spanish composer and guitarist whose father was also a guitarist. It is said that when his father was at work, he would play his guitar and try to imitate the beautiful sounds he had heard. Tárrega became the patriarch of an enormously influential group of guitarists who, building on his methods and ideas, exerted great influence over the development of the guitar in the 20th century.